THE SUBTLE DECEPTION OF PRIDE

Help Me

I'm Falling!

CHARLES R. SUND

Help Me I'm Falling!
© 2010 by Charles R. Sund

Published by Insight Publishing Group
4739 E. 91st Street, Suite 210
Tulsa, OK 74137
918-493-1718

All rights reserved. No part of this book may be reproduced or transmitted in any form or by any means, electronic or mechanical, including photocopying and recording, or by an information storage and retrieval system, without permission in writing from the author.

Unless otherwise noted all Scripture quotations are taken from the *New King James Version* of the Bible unless otherwise noted. Copyright © 1979, 1980, 1982, Thomas Nelson, Inc., Publishers.

The scripture quotation marked AMP is taken from *The Amplified Bible, New Testament,* copyright © 1958, 1987 by The Lockman Foundation, La Habra, California.

The scripture quotations marked KJV are taken from the *King James Version* of the Bible.

ISBN: 978-1-932503-95-1

Library of Congress catalog card number: 2010936156

Printed in the United States of America

DEDICATION

I'd like to dedicate this book to my awesome Lord and Savior, Jesus Christ; my beautiful wife, Nancy of thirty-nine years; and last but not least, to my mother and all those who prayed me out of darkness and into the marvelous light of the Gospel of Jesus Christ.

I love you and appreciate you very much!

CONTENTS

Acknowledgements	7
Introduction	9
The Definition of "Pride"	11
Chapter 1 Two Visions	13
I. Vision of Local Church	13
II. Vision of the Hand	14
Chapter 2 The Fall of Lucifer	17
Chapter 3 The Fall of Man	27
Chapter 4 The Subtlety of Pride	39
Chapter 5 Results of a Prideful Heart	49
Chapter 6 Safeguarding Our Hearts from the Sin of Pride	61
Closing Thoughts	71
Christian Prayer	75
Sinner's Prayer	77
Scripture References	79
About the Author	81

Acknowledgements

I would like to acknowledge RHEMA Bible Training Center, my book editor, Connie Holmen and all of my fellow Christian ministers and friends who have encouraged me all these years to never give up.

Introduction

The purpose of this book is to awaken the Christian (particularly those in leadership positions) to the oldest, most subtle, dangerous and destructive weapon in satan's arsenal; the weapon of (Deception by Pride).

I've heard it said that if a deceived person knew they were deceived, they wouldn't be deceived; meaning that if we knew just how dangerous and destructive pride really is, we would do everything possible to guard our hearts against it.

Humility is God's way of exaltation and it will cause us to stand as we run our race, not a false humility but a godly humility that actually strengthens us and causes us to remain teachable while we are serving God and others.

God is calling all of His people to humility which is what we do as an act of our will. James 4 verse 10 says for us to; Humble ourselves in the sight of the Lord and He will lift us up.

Many a Christian leader and member of the Body of Christ have fallen prey to satan's weapon of deception by pride. At times, we've put ourselves in places of position wanting to be served instead of being a servant. Satan knows that if he can get us to exalt ourselves, the door for destruction and cause for a fall have now been opened.

The Bible says in Proverbs 16 verse 18 that Pride comes before destruction and a haughty spirit before a fall.

This book of course is based upon much scripture and also reveals two visions given to me by God in order to cause us to further understand the seriousness of this subject matter.

I pray that as you read *Help Me I'm Falling!*, you will open up your heart and allow the precious Holy Spirit to reveal any areas of pride in your life that have caused you to exalt yourself, hindering your walk with God and with others. Then, I sincerely pray that you will do as Apostle Peter said in 1st Peter 5 verse 6; Humble yourself under the Mighty Hand of God that He may exalt you in due time.

P.S. This book is Not meant to condemn anyone who has possibly fallen because of pride, but it is meant to stir all of our hearts towards humility.

Sincerely in His Service,
Charles R. Sund

The Definition of "Pride"

Hebrew meaning: To grow tall, be high, to rise up; by extension: to be exalted: proud, arrogant, conceit, haughtiness, swelling, resurrection.[1]

Greek meaning: To envelope or cover like smoke, to inflate with self-conceit, to be highly misled, to be lifted up, to be proved, make a smoke, slowly consume without flame, arrogance, presumption, braggart, boaster.[2]

Webster's: Arrogance, loftiness, conceit, smugness, to value oneself, taken credit, glory, complacency, exaggerated self-esteem, an unduly high opinion of oneself.

---

[1] James Strong, LL.D., S.T.D., "Hebrew and Aramaic Dictionary of the Old Testament," *The Strongest Strong's Exhaustive Concordance of the Bible,* Zondervan Publishers, 1843, #1342, #1343, #1346, #1347.

[2] James Strong, LL.D., S.T.D., "Hebrew and Aramaic Dictionary of the Old Testament," *The Strongest Strong's Exhaustive Concordance of the Bible,* Zondervan Publishers, 1843 #1361, #1363; 1986 #212, #213; 2069 #5187; 2070 #5243.

CHAPTER 1
Two Visions

I. Vision of Local Church

This first vision came to me in the year 1990 as I was seeking the Lord concerning the increase of deception that I had noticed in the local church and the Body of Christ.

I had begun to notice a lack of reverence for the Lord resulting particularly in sinful "Christian" lifestyles. This troubled me, especially seeing those in leadership living lifestyles of compromise. I wondered how this could be. Preaching the holy Word of God behind the pulpit, but living a compromised life during the week. Not that God expects us to be perfect, but He does expect us, <u>especially</u> as leaders, to set a good, godly example.

I questioned in my mind, wondering if they just didn't see that the way they were living their life was wrong or if they just didn't realize the seriousness of it. I began to seek the Lord about these matters; things that they were doing that weren't setting a good example and were not pleasing to God.

As I was praying in the spirit one afternoon concerning these matters, all of a sudden I had what would be called an open vision. My eyes were open.

In this vision I saw buildings falling to the ground; it seemed as if in slow motion as the walls began to crumble; others falling instantly to the ground. I remember it so vividly as the dust from the piles of rubble shot out from beneath.

At once this vision was over. The next thing I remember was asking the Lord what this vision was all about and if it was from Him. I asked the Holy Spirit to reveal the meaning of it to me. I sat down in a chair in our living room to get quiet before the Lord, and immediately the Holy Spirit spoke to me and said, "These are local churches. They are falling because of their pride. Those ministers who refuse to repent of their pride, I will remove them from their pulpits, but those who repent of their pride, I will allow them to remain." Then the Holy Spirit took me on a tour through the scriptures to confirm the vision.

I'll never forget as I simply flipped my Bible open. It opened to Obadiah 1, and there in verse 3, which jumped out at me, it said, *"The pride of your heart has deceived you."* This answered my question to God of how deception was getting into the church. Then the Lord began to take me through the scriptures in my mind starting with the fall of Lucifer and the fall of man.

II. Vision of the Hand

The second vision came to me in the year 1999 as I was praying in the spirit. In this vision my eyes were closed and I saw a man standing at the threshold of heaven wondering why he wasn't allowed to enter. There was a huge hand resisting him. He was getting extremely frustrated and began to panic and cry out saying repeatedly, "Why can't I come in? Please let me in." Then I heard the voice of the one resisting him say, "Because you have on the wrong clothes. You're trying to get in your own way."

Then, the vision was over, but the Lord said to me, "Even in the natural realm there in the earth, there are certain establishments which won't allow you to enter unless you have on the proper clothing!" I remember replying, saying, "You're right, Lord; that is true."

Then to confirm this vision, the Holy Spirit quickened me to read 1 Peter 5:5-6:

> *⁵Likewise you younger people, submit yourselves to your elders. Yes, all of you be submissive to one another, and be (clothed with humility), for "God <u>resists</u> the proud, but <u>gives grace</u> to the humble." ⁶Therefore (humble yourselves) under the <u>mighty hand</u> of God, that He may exalt you in due time.*

He began to talk to me about the fact that many of His people need a change of clothing. They need to change their clothes spiritually speaking. He said they needed to take off their clothes of pride and put on clothes of humility.

CHAPTER 2

THE FALL OF LUCIFER

The Bible says in Philippians 2:10-11 that there is coming a day when every knee will bow and every tongue will confess that Jesus Christ is Lord.

In 1980 when I first knew that I was called to preach, I heard the Lord say to me, *"Son, I want you to always pray and ask Me to help you stay humble before Me so that I can use you in a mighty way in the last days."* I'll never forget those words. They were embedded in my spirit. We all must realize that we live in a world filled with ungodly pride because of the fallen and sinful nature of man.

We must realize first of all that Lucifer (Satan) wants us to fall. He wants to take us out of the presence of God just as he was and is. Lucifer knows that if he can get us to exalt ourselves in our own hearts and minds, we will end up deceived and eventually fall. After all, he knows exactly how it works because that is exactly what happened to him and he paid an awful price for it. No longer was he satisfied with <u>serving</u> God in God's Kingdom. He became hungry for more power and recognition. He wasn't satisfied any more with his present notoriety and place of authority in the Kingdom of which God his Creator was so gracious to let him live, dwell and enjoy.

Lucifer's downfall began as he began to look upon his own beauty and accomplishments, not realizing that his (self-exaltation) would only bring him low and to ruin, desolation, separation from God and eventually destruction. He began to be lifted up in his heart, thinking more highly of himself than he ought to think. His contentment to serve in the Kingdom began to wane and thoughts began to flood his mind; thoughts of the possibility of taking the place of God and becoming like God Himself. He no longer had a humble heart and attitude of a servant, but had fallen in love with his own beauty and ended up in a state of ungodly pride and self-centeredness.

Now, instead of being content to serve in the Kingdom of his Creator, he wanted to be served. Instead of being a follower, he wanted to be followed. His attitude had changed which affected not only his life and status, but the life and status of one-third of heaven's angelic hosts. They ended up following him and falling with him.

Jude 1:6:

⁶And the angels who did not keep their proper domain, but left their own abode, He has reserved in everlasting chains under darkness for the judgment of the great day.

Think about that! One-third of the angels ended up deceived. So we see by this example that along with truth, deception also has a following. What a sad day it must have been for the Lord to see this happen, to see wrong choices being made. Choices that would affect the very Kingdom of heaven itself and its Kingdom order.

You see, Lucifer's fall began when he took his eyes off of God and fixed them on himself. That's how pride began. In other words, pride didn't start with pride, just as strife doesn't start with strife. There were other things that took place which led to pride and strife. He, Lucifer, began to look upon himself and how beautiful and talented he was, apparently forgetting that his beauty and talents were given to him by God and for the glory of God! This is where man gets into trouble and begins to receive the glory for himself.

We read in Isaiah 14:12-14:

[12]How you are fallen from heaven, O Lucifer, son of the morning. How you are cut down to the ground, you who weakened the nations! [13]For you have said in your heart: I will ascend into heaven, I will exalt my throne above the stars of God; I will also sit on the mount of the congregation on the farthest sides of the north; [14]I will ascend above the heights of the cloud; I will be like the Most High.

In this passage of scripture, you can see that pride had filled his heart as he stated five times, *I will*. In other words, Lucifer was saying, "By an act of my will (my free will to choose), I choose to exalt myself!"

Don't ever forget this! The Big I is always a result of pride that enters our heart. Remember what Jesus said in Luke 22:42? *"Not My will, but Yours* (His Father's) *be done."*

Always be careful about the Big I. Watch out for the Big I. Did you ever notice that the letter "i" is the middle letter in the word "pride"? I thought this to be interesting. That brings me to another passage of scripture that goes along with the subject of pride.

It's found in 1 Samuel 15:10-17 KJV:

¹⁰Then came the word of the LORD unto Samuel, saying, ¹¹It repenteth me that I have set up Saul to be king: for he is turned back from following me, and hath not performed my commandments. And it grieved Samuel; and he cried unto the LORD all night. ¹²And when Samuel rose early to meet Saul in the morning, it was told Samuel, saying, Saul came to Carmel, and, behold, he set him up a place, and is gone about, and passed on, and gone down to Gilgal. ¹³And Samuel came to Saul: and Saul said unto him, Blessed be thou of the LORD: I have performed the commandment of the LORD. ¹⁴And Samuel said, What meaneth then this bleating of the sheep in mine ears, and the lowing of the oxen which I hear? ¹⁵And Saul said, They have brought them from the Amalekites: for the people spared the best of the sheep and of the oxen, to sacrifice unto the LORD thy God; and the rest we have utterly destroyed. ¹⁶Then Samuel said unto Saul, Stay, and I will tell thee what the LORD hath said to me this night. And he said unto him, Say on. ¹⁷And Samuel said, When thou wast little in thine own sight, wast thou not made the head of the tribes of Israel, and the LORD anointed thee king over Israel?

Notice verse 11. Saul turned back from following God. What happened? What caused Saul to turn away from God? The answer is found in verse 17. Saul didn't stay small in his own eyes, in his own estimation. He didn't remember from whence he came. He decided to do things his own way and ended up disobeying the Lord's instructions by not destroying and consuming the sinners and Amalekites.

1 Samuel 15:18-23 kjv:

[18]And the LORD sent thee on a journey, and said, Go and utterly destroy the sinners the Amalekites, and fight against them until they be consumed. [19]Wherefore then didst thou not obey the voice of the LORD, but didst fly upon the spoil, and didst evil in the sight of the LORD? [20]And Saul said unto Samuel, Yea, I have obeyed the voice of the LORD, and have gone the way which the LORD sent me, and have brought Agag the king of Amalek, and have utterly destroyed the Amalekites. [21]But the people took of the spoil, sheep and oxen, the chief of the things which should have been utterly destroyed, to sacrifice unto the LORD thy God in Gilgal.

[22]And Samuel said, Hath the LORD as great delight in burnt offerings and sacrifices, as in obeying the voice of the LORD? Behold, to obey is better than sacrifice, and to hearken than the fat of rams. [23]For rebellion is as the sin of witchcraft, and stubbornness is as iniquity and idolatry. Because thou hast rejected the word of the LORD, he hath also rejected thee from being king.

So because of Saul's pride, he ended up rebelling against God's words to him. (Always remember that rebellion and stubbornness against God's Word are a direct result of pride in our lives; and if we refuse to repent, we will be resisted by God Himself.)

1 Peter 5:5:

[5]Likewise you younger people, submit yourselves to your elders. Yes, all of you be submissive to one another, and be

clothed with _humility,_ for "God _resists_ the proud, but _gives grace_ to the humble."

At one time, Saul was a humble man, a humble Christian we could say, and a humble leader. He was small in his own eyes, but he didn't remain that way. He let the Big I get in the way and it cost him his leadership position. God loved Saul but was not pleased with Saul and had to deal with his pride. Saul's pride brought him low, **not God!**

Notice some of the results which stem from the root of pride in this story. Saul said in verse 20, *"But I have obeyed the voice of the* Lord [and] *utterly destroyed the Amalekites!*

Unrepented pride will eventually produce lying and blaming others.

Notice in 1 Samuel 15:24 KJV:

And Saul said unto Samuel, I have sinned: for I have transgressed the commandment of the Lord, and thy words: because I feared the people, and obeyed their voice.

It wasn't until _after_ Saul heard that he lost his kingship that he admitted he sinned by not fully obeying the Lord's instructions. But, thank God that he did repent. (Always remember that when you slip over into the sin of pride, be quick to repent and humble yourself when the Holy Spirit reveals pride to you, and He will!)

Remember to stay small in your own eyes and to never cover or hide your sin, because it will always resurface at a later time. In verse 24 Saul said that he feared the people, which was true because Proverbs 29:25 says that *the fear of man brings a snare,* and we know Saul became snared.

The fear of man will cause you and me to obey man's plans and purposes instead of God's plans and purposes. The fear of man must be overcome in our lives if we're going to wholly follow the Lord. Read Joshua 14:8-9, 14. These particular scriptures talk about wholly following the Lord.

> *⁸Nevertheless my brethren who went up with me made the heart of the people melt, but I wholly followed the LORD my God. ⁹So Moses swore on that day, saying, "Surely the land where your foot has trodden shall be your inheritance and your children's forever, because you have wholly followed the LORD my God." ¹⁴Hebron therefore became the inheritance of Caleb the son of Jephunneh the Kenizzite to this day, because he wholly followed the LORD God of Israel.*

In Galatians 1:10 Paul says, *"Do I now persuade man or God; or do I seek to please man? For if I still please men, I would not be a bond servant of Christ."*

Saul became a man pleaser and it cost him his leadership position.

Having pastored two churches, let me particularly encourage all pastors and leaders to be God fearing, not man fearing. True, godly fear and humility always submit to God's way of doing things and not man's. Don't give into the pressures of the expectations of man. Whatever <u>God</u> says, just do it and don't be afraid of what others might say, think or do.

Ezekiel 3:1-11:

> *¹Moreover He said to me, "Son of man, eat what you find; eat this scroll, and go, speak to the house of Israel." ²So I opened my mouth, and He caused me to eat that scroll.*

³And He said to me, "Son of man, feed your belly, and fill your stomach with this scroll that I give you." So I ate, and it was in my mouth like honey in sweetness. ⁴Then He said to me: "Son of man, go to the house of Israel and speak with My words to them. ⁵For you are not sent to a people of unfamiliar speech and of hard language, but to the house of Israel, ⁶not to many people of unfamiliar speech and of hard language, whose words you cannot understand. Surely, had I sent you to them, they would have listened to you. ⁷But the house of Israel will not listen to you, because they will not listen to Me; for all the house of Israel are impudent and hard-hearted. ⁸Behold, I have made your face strong against their faces, and your forehead strong against their foreheads. ⁹Like adamant stone, harder than flint, I have made your forehead; do not be afraid of them, nor be dismayed at their looks, though they are a rebellious house."

¹⁰<u>Moreover He said to me: "Son of man, receive into your heart all My words that I speak to you, and hear with your ears.</u> ¹¹And go, get to the captives, to the children of your people, and speak to them and tell them, 'Thus says the Lord GOD,' whether they hear, or whether they refuse."

We will all individually stand before <u>God, not man</u>, to give account of what we did for God here on this earth.

The fear of man seeks to paralyze God's people, particularly those in leadership positions. It wants to keep us from speaking the truth and moving forward with God and brings with it much confusion which leads to compromise.

I know what I'm talking about! I've experienced the pressure of people's opinions, and it seems like everyone has their own opinion about things. I've come to realize, however, that God is not interested in our opinions, but He is interested in His Word. Therefore, He does not seek the opinions of men concerning His will, whether we should do His will or not. <u>He seeks our obedience to His will.</u>

Acts 5:29 says, *"But Peter and the other apostles said: 'We ought to obey God rather than men.'"* Don't let the devil of fear rule your decision-making process. Proverbs 14:26 says, *"In <u>the fear of the LORD there is strong confidence. And his children will have a place of refuge.</u>"* You and I will never have strong confidence if we are continually concerned about the opinions of others more than God's Word.

If Saul would have maintained a fear of God in his life, he wouldn't have given in to the pressures of the fear of man. What a lesson this is for us to learn and to learn quickly. There is great freedom in the fear of the Lord.

Proverbs 1:7 says, *"The fear of the Lord is the beginning of knowledge; but fools despise wisdom and instruction."*

You see, brothers and sisters in Christ, when we are walking humbly before God, we will do what He wants us to do, not what others think we should do. Yes, the Bible does say in Proverbs 11:14, *"Where there is no counsel, the people fall; but in the multitude of counselors there is safety."* However, when you <u>know</u> that God has told you to do something, you do not ask others if you should do it. That would be the same as saying to God, "God, do You want me to do what You're telling me to do or what my friends think I should do?" Or it would be like asking God if we should obey Him.

Let me ask you a question! Did Moses seek the <u>approval</u> of others when God told him to go down to Egypt and deliver

God's people? **No!** Did Abraham seek the <u>approval</u> of those around him when God put it in his heart to separate himself from Lot? **No!** Did Saul (Paul) seek the approval of the other disciples when God told him to preach the message of salvation to the Gentiles? **No!** Did Jesus ask those around Him if they thought He should die for mankind? **No!** Why? Because they all heard from God and were not concerned about man's approval, and they had a greater fear of obeying God than of obeying man.

Remember this: Pride obeys man and humility obeys God directly and obeys God's instructions to man through man. Also, we cannot truly say that we as God's people are submitted to God if we are not submitted to those whom God has placed in authority over us.

Allow me to confirm this to you scripturally.

Hebrews 13:7 KJV:

[7]Remember those which have the rule over you, who have spoken unto you the word of God: whose faith (not personality) follow, considering the end of their conversation.

Hebrews 13:17 KJV:

[17]<u>Obey</u> them that have the <u>rule</u> over you, and <u>submit</u> yourselves: for they <u>watch for your souls</u>, as they that must give account, that they may do it with joy, and not with grief: for that is unprofitable for you.

CHAPTER 3
THE FALL OF MAN

Genesis, chapter 3:

THE TEMPTATION AND FALL OF MAN

¹Now the serpent was more cunning than any beast of the field which the LORD God had made. And he said to the woman, "Has God indeed said, 'You shall not eat of every tree of the garden'?" ²And the woman said to the serpent, "We may eat the fruit of the trees of the garden; ³but of the fruit of the tree which is in the midst of the garden, God has said, 'You shall not eat it, nor shall you touch it, lest you die.'" ⁴Then the serpent said to the woman, "You will not surely die. ⁵For God knows that in the day you eat of it your eyes will be opened, and you will be like God, knowing good and evil." ⁶So when the woman saw that the tree was good for food, that it was pleasant to the eyes, and a tree desirable to make one wise, she took of its fruit and ate. She also gave to her husband with her, and he ate. ⁷Then the eyes of both of them were opened, and they knew that they were naked; and they sewed fig leaves together and made themselves coverings. ⁸And they heard the sound of the LORD God walking in the garden in the cool of the day, and Adam and his wife hid themselves from the presence of the LORD God among the trees of the garden. ⁹Then the LORD God called to Adam and said to him, "Where are you?"

¹⁰So he said, "I heard Your voice in the garden, and I was afraid because I was naked; and I hid myself."

¹¹And He said, "Who told you that you were naked? Have you eaten from the tree of which I commanded you that you should not eat?"

¹²Then the man said, "The woman whom You gave to be with me, she gave me of the tree, and I ate."

¹³And the LORD God said to the woman, "What is this you have done?"

The woman said, "The serpent deceived me, and I ate."

¹⁴So the LORD God said to the serpent:

"Because you have done this,
You are cursed more than all cattle,
And more than every beast of the field;
On your belly you shall go,
And you shall eat dust
All the days of your life.

¹⁵And I will put enmity
Between you and the woman,
And between your seed and her Seed;
He shall bruise your head,
And you shall bruise His heel."

¹⁶To the woman He said:

"I will greatly multiply your sorrow and your conception; in pain you shall bring forth children;
Your desire shall be for your husband,

And he shall rule over you."
[17]*Then to Adam He said, "Because you have heeded the voice of your wife, and have eaten from the tree of which I commanded you, saying, 'You shall not eat of it':*

"Cursed is the ground for your sake;
In toil you shall eat of it
All the days of your life.

[18]*Both thorns and thistles it shall bring forth for you,*
And you shall eat the herb of the field. [19]*In the sweat of your face you shall eat bread*

Till you return to the ground,
For out of it you were taken;
For dust you are,
And to dust you shall return."

[20]*And Adam called his wife's name Eve, because she was the mother of all living.*
[21]*Also for Adam and his wife the LORD God made tunics of skin, and clothed them.*
[22]*Then the LORD God said, "Behold, the man has become like one of Us, to know good and evil. And now, lest he put out his hand and take also of the tree of life, and eat, and live forever"—* [23]*therefore the LORD God sent him out of the garden of Eden to till the ground from which he was taken.* [24]*So He drove out the man; and He placed cherubim at the east of the garden of Eden, and a flaming sword which turned every way, to guard the way to the tree of life.*

As we read the account of the fall of man (Adam and Eve) in Genesis 3, we will come to understand that it was their pride that caused them to fall and lose their position of authority. "But I thought they fell because they disobeyed God by partaking of the fruit of the tree of knowledge of good and evil." Yes, that's right, but what caused them to disobey? What caused them to disobey was that they decided to do things their own way.

Remember the Big I! "So you mean to tell me that it wasn't the serpent (Lucifer) who caused them to fall?" That's right! We must realize that the only thing the serpent could do was tempt them to disobey God. He couldn't make them disobey God. That was Adam and Eve's choice.

Remember, God gave them dominion (authority) over everything that creepeth upon the earth. That included the serpent.

Genesis 1:26, 28:

[26]Then God said, "Let Us make man in Our image, according to Our likeness; let them have dominion over the fish of the sea, over the birds of the air, and over the cattle, over all the earth and over every creeping thing that creeps on the earth." [28]Then God blessed them, and God said to them, "Be fruitful and multiply; fill the earth and subdue it; have dominion over the fish of the sea, over the birds of the air, and over every living thing that moves on the earth."

However, because they decided to do things their way, they lost their God-given place of authority. They, Adam and Eve, through their disobedience, delivered their authority to the serpent (Lucifer, the devil and our enemy). They gave in to the temptation of the lust of the eyes and ended up deceived. That would tell us then that if we don't give into the devil's temptations of pride, we'll stay out of the sin of pride and maintain our position of authority over Satan.

Temptation in and of itself is not sin. In other words, just because Satan tempts us doesn't mean we have sinned. It's when we yield to his temptations and fall into them that it becomes sin.

I think we can all agree that Satan is good at what he does and because he is now the god of <u>this world</u>, he has the authority to tempt us to sin, but thank God he doesn't have the authority to make us sin. He can tempt us to exalt ourselves, but he can't make us exalt ourselves. That is great news! Hallelujah!

2 Corinthians 4:3-4 KJV:

³But if our gospel be hid, it is hid to them that are lost: ⁴In whom the god of this world hath blinded the minds of them which believe not, lest the light of the glorious gospel of Christ, who is the image of God, should shine unto them.

Are you telling me that as a Christian I don't have to sin? That's exactly right; you don't have to sin, and if you and I use our God-given authority and resist Satan's temptations to sin, we will stay out of sin.

I have found in my life that Satan, the serpent, is extremely subtle, but that when I stay filled with the Word of God and the Holy Spirit, I am sensitive to the Holy Spirit and the warnings of Satan's temptations of pride. Thank God for the precious Holy Spirit who shows us things to come and gives us the power to overcome every one of Satan's temptations. You and I just need to be more cunning than Satan, and we can be. Satan tempts us with thoughts of pride (self- exaltation). He knows that if he can get us to exalt ourselves, we will fall and eventually be destroyed.

Proverbs 16:18:

¹⁸Pride goes before destruction, and a haughty spirit before a fall.

After all, that's exactly what happened to Lucifer. No wonder he tempts us with prideful thoughts and actions.

Some of you may remember the famous phrase or line spoken by comedian Flip Wilson. "The devil made me do it!" No, Flip, the devil didn't make you do it. He tempted you to do it, and by an act of your free will, you chose to do it.

Both Adam and Eve were present when the Lord instructed them not to eat of the tree of life, the tree of knowledge of good and evil. They heard what their God said. Just as when Lucifer fell, I'm sure God must have been saddened to see what Adam and Eve had done. All God ever wanted for them was good and for them to see good, but once they partook of the fruit of the tree of the knowledge of good and evil, their eyes were suddenly opened to see evil. Their act of disobedience and rebellion against God interrupted God's plan, but thank God, He (God) had another plan.

Has this ever happened to you? Has God's plan for your life ever been interrupted by your plan? It has happened to me and I am sure to all of us, but thank God for His forgiveness, mercy and grace to help us get back on the track of humility. He is such a loving and compassionate Father who always forgives us when we ask and never holds our sins against us.

There have been times in my life when I blew it big time and wasn't sure if He would get me out of the mess I made. But I've come to know His love for me in a greater way. A revelation of His love has given me the confidence I need concerning the fact that even though I've messed up BIG at times, He is bigger than my big mess and is there to help me, forgive me and bring me through. Pride says, "I know what God told me, but I want to do it my way anyway."

Do you remember Frank Sinatra's hit song, "I Did It My Way"? Don't forget about the Big I! The Big I will always cause us to fall, to bring us down.

So Adam and Eve, because they decided to do things their own way, fell from their God-given place of authority as did King Saul.

Samson was another example of the fall of pride. He was a mighty man blessed of God until he took matters into his own hands and became unequally yoked to a Philistine harlot woman named Delilah.

SAMSON AND DELILAH

Judges, chapter 16:

[1]Now Samson went to Gaza and saw a harlot there, and went in to her. [2]When the Gazites were told, "Samson has come here!" they surrounded the place and lay in wait for him all night at the gate of the city. They were quiet all night, saying, "In the morning, when it is daylight, we will kill him." [3]And Samson lay low till midnight; then he arose at midnight, took hold of the doors of the gate of the city and the two gateposts, pulled them up, bar and all, put them on his shoulders, and carried them to the top of the hill that faces Hebron. [4]Afterward it happened that he loved a woman in the Valley of Sorek, whose name was Delilah. [5]And the

lords of the Philistines came up to her and said to her, "Entice him, and find out where his great strength lies, and by what means we may overpower him, that we may bind him to afflict him; and every one of us will give you eleven hundred pieces of silver."

⁶So Delilah said to Samson, "Please tell me where your great strength lies, and with what you may be bound to afflict you."

⁷And Samson said to her, "If they bind me with seven fresh bowstrings, not yet dried, then I shall become weak, and be like any other man."

⁸So the lords of the Philistines brought up to her seven fresh bowstrings, not yet dried, and she bound him with them. ⁹Now men were lying in wait, staying with her in the room. And she said to him, "The Philistines are upon you, Samson!" But he broke the bowstrings as a strand of yarn breaks when it touches fire. So the secret of his strength was not known.

¹⁰Then Delilah said to Samson, "Look, you have mocked me and told me lies. Now, please tell me what you may be bound with."

¹¹So he said to her, "If they bind me securely with new ropes that have never been used, then I shall become weak, and be like any other man."

¹²Therefore Delilah took new ropes and bound him with them, and said to him, "The Philistines are upon you, Samson!" And men were lying in wait, staying in the room. But he broke them off his arms like a thread.

¹³Delilah said to Samson, "Until now you have mocked me and told me lies. Tell me what you may be bound with." And he said to her, "If you weave the seven locks of my head into the web of the loom"—

14So she wove it tightly with the batten of the loom, and said to him, "The Philistines are upon you, Samson!" But he awoke from his sleep, and pulled out the batten and the web from the loom.

15Then she said to him, "How can you say, 'I love you,' when your heart is not with me? You have mocked me these three times, and have not told me where your great strength lies." 16And it came to pass, when she pestered him daily with her words and pressed him, so that his soul was vexed to death, 17that he told her all his heart, and said to her, "No razor has ever come upon my head, for I have been a Nazirite to God from my mother's womb. If I am shaven, then my strength will leave me, and I shall become weak, and be like any other man."

18When Delilah saw that he had told her all his heart, she sent and called for the lords of the Philistines, saying, "Come up once more, for he has told me all his heart." So the lords of the Philistines came up to her and brought the money in their hand. 19Then she lulled him to sleep on her knees, and called for a man and had him shave off the seven locks of his head. Then she began to torment him, and his strength left him. 20And she said, "The Philistines are upon you, Samson!" So he awoke from his sleep, and said, "I will go out as before, at other times, and shake myself free!" But he did not know that the LORD had departed from him.

21Then the Philistines took him and put out his eyes, and brought him down to Gaza. They bound him with bronze fetters, and he became a grinder in the prison. 22However, the hair of his head began to grow again after it had been shaven.

Samson Dies with the Philistines

²³Now the lords of the Philistines gathered together to offer a great sacrifice to Dagon their god, and to rejoice. And they said:

"Our god has delivered into our hands
Samson our enemy!"

²⁴When the people saw him, they praised their god; for they said: "Our god has delivered into our hands our enemy, The destroyer of our land,
And the one who multiplied our dead."

²⁵So it happened, when their hearts were merry, that they said, "Call for Samson, that he may perform for us." So they called for Samson from the prison, and he performed for them. And they stationed him between the pillars. ²⁶Then Samson said to the lad who held him by the hand, "Let me feel the pillars which support the temple, so that I can lean on them." ²⁷Now the temple was full of men and women. All the lords of the Philistines were there—about three thousand men and women on the roof watching while Samson performed.

²⁸Then Samson called to the LORD, saying, "O Lord GOD, remember me, I pray! Strengthen me, I pray, just this once, O God, that I may with one blow take vengeance on the Philistines for my two eyes!" ²⁹And Samson took hold of the two middle pillars which supported the temple, and he braced himself against them, one on his right and the other on his left. ³⁰Then Samson said, "Let me die with the Philistines!" And he pushed with all his might, and the temple fell on the lords and all the people who were in it. So the dead that he killed at his death were more than he had killed in his life.

[31]And his brothers and all his father's household came down and took him, and brought him up and buried him between Zorah and Eshtaol in the tomb of his father Manoah. He had judged Israel twenty years.

It reminds me of some of the great leaders and powerful men and women of God of the past and of today who have fallen prey to Satan's seducing tactics.

Did God bring these leaders or individuals down? NO! Did God cause them to fall? NO! Their own pride brought them low. Their own self-will. Did God still love them? YES, YES, YES!

I know that in this book, I repeat certain phrases. I don't mean to be redundant, but this is a serious message for a serious time that we're living in. If the writing of this book can help even one Christian, or Christian leader in the Body of Christ, stay out of pride and remain humble so they can run their race and finish their course, it will be worth it.

CHAPTER 4

THE SUBTLETY OF PRIDE

We know through the fall of Adam and Eve just how subtle Satan, the serpent, was and still is. Ephesians 6:11 tells us to *"Put on the whole armour of God, that you and I may be able to stand against the wiles* (scheming, craftiness, strategy) *of the devil."* Satan is ever scheming in order to tempt man to exalt himself so he can bring man low. He continually strategizes on how he can trip us up and cause us to fall.

Ezekiel 28:1-19:

¹The word of the LORD came to me again, saying, ²"Son of man, say to the prince of Tyre, 'Thus says the Lord GOD:

"Because your heart is lifted up, and you say, 'I am a god, I sit in the seat of gods, in the midst of the seas' yet you are a man, and not a god, Though you set your heart as the heart of a god ³(Behold, you are wiser than Daniel! There is no secret that can be hidden from you!
⁴With your wisdom and your understanding You have gained riches for yourself,
    and gathered gold and silver into your treasuries;

⁵By your great wisdom in trade you have increased your riches, and your heart is lifted up because of your riches),"
⁶"Therefore thus says the Lord GOD:

"Because you have set your heart as the heart of a god, ⁷Behold, therefore, I will bring strangers against you, the most terrible of the nations; and they shall draw their swords against the beauty of your wisdom, and defile your splendor. ⁸They shall throw you down into the Pit, and you shall die the death of the slain in the midst of the seas.
⁹"Will you still say before him who slays you, 'I am a god'?

But you shall be a man, and not a god, in the hand of him who slays you.
¹⁰You shall die the death of the uncircumcised

By the hand of aliens; for I have spoken," says the Lord GOD.'"

Lamentation for the King of Tyre

¹¹Moreover the word of the LORD came to me, saying, ¹²"Son of man, take up a lamentation for the king of Tyre, and say to him, 'Thus says the Lord GOD:

" You were the seal of perfection,
Full of wisdom and perfect in beauty.
¹³You were in Eden, the garden of God;
Every precious stone was your covering:
The sardius, topaz, and diamond,
Beryl, onyx, and jasper,
Sapphire, turquoise, and emerald with gold.
The workmanship of your timbrels and pipes
Was prepared for you on the day you were created.

[14]"You were the anointed cherub who covers; I established you; You were on the holy mountain of God; You walked back and forth in the midst of fiery stones.
[15]You were perfect in your ways from the day you were created, till iniquity was found in you.
[16]By the abundance of your trading
   You became filled with violence within,
   And you sinned; Therefore I cast you as a profane thing, out of the mountain of God;
   And I destroyed you, O covering cherub,
   From the midst of the fiery stones.
[17]Your heart was lifted up because of your beauty; you corrupted your wisdom for the sake of your splendor; I cast you to the ground, I laid you before kings, that they might gaze at you.
[18]You defiled your sanctuaries
   By the multitude of your iniquities,
   By the iniquity of your trading;
   Therefore I brought fire from your midst;
   It devoured you, and I turned you to ashes upon the earth in the sight of all who saw you.
[19]All who knew you among the peoples are astonished at you; You have become a horror, and shall be no more forever."'"

Isaiah 14:12:

[12]"How you are fallen from heaven, O Lucifer, son of the morning! How you are cut down to the ground, you who weakened the nations!"

Luke 10:18:

[18]And He said to them, "I saw Satan fall like lightning from heaven."

Satan knows that he was thrown out of heaven and that his time is short.

Revelation 12:12:

¹²"Therefore rejoice, O heavens, and you who dwell in them! Woe to the inhabitants of the earth and the sea! For the devil has come down to you, having great wrath, because he knows that he has a short time."

His only way to get back at God is by getting to us.

John 10:10:

¹⁰The thief does not come except to steal, and to kill, and to destroy. I have come that they may have life, and that they may have it more abundantly.

Satan hates anything that has to do with life, because God is life and the Life Giver of every living thing. Satan comes to snuff the life out of us and destroy us. One thing he uses to destroy us is pride. Pride cometh before what? Before destruction!

In order to better understand what caused Lucifer's fall and how his heart ended up the way it did (corrupt and sinful), let's read Ezekiel 28:11-19 KJV again. Most theologians today believe that this text refers to Satan's fall.

¹¹Moreover the word of the LORD came unto me, saying, ¹²Son of man, take up a lamentation upon the king of Tyrus, and say unto him, Thus saith the Lord GOD; Thou sealest up the sum, full of wisdom, and perfect in beauty. ¹³Thou hast been in Eden the garden of God; every precious stone was thy covering, the sardius, topaz, and the diamond, the beryl, the onyx, and the jasper, the sapphire, the emerald, and the carbuncle, and gold: the workmanship of thy tabrets and of thy pipes was prepared in thee in the day that thou wast created. ¹⁴Thou art the anointed cherub that covereth; and I have set thee so: thou wast upon the holy mountain of God; thou hast walked up and down in the midst of the stones of fire. ¹⁵Thou wast perfect in thy ways from the day that thou wast created, till iniquity (wrong, evil, sin, injustice, warped, twisted, perverted, wicked, unrighteous) *was found in thee. ¹⁶By the multitude of thy merchandise they have filled the midst of thee with violence, and thou hast sinned: therefore I will cast thee as profane out of the mountain of God: and I will destroy thee, O covering cherub, from the midst of the stones of fire. ¹⁷Thine heart was lifted up* (pride) *because of thy beauty, thou hast corrupted thy wisdom by reason of thy brightness: I will cast thee to the ground, I will lay thee before kings, that they may behold thee. ¹⁸Thou hast defiled thy sanctuaries by the multitude of thine iniquities, by the iniquity of thy traffick* (trading of merchandise); *therefore will I bring forth a fire from the midst of thee, it shall devour thee, and I will bring thee to ashes upon the earth in the sight of all them that behold thee. ¹⁹All they that know thee among the people shall be astonished at thee: thou shalt be a terror, and never shalt thou be any more.*

Notice: Lucifer corrupted his God-given wisdom for the sake of his splendor or beauty. In other words, he let his beauty and splendor go to his head and from there into his heart. This caused him to corrupt the wisdom God gave him. He let his beauty and splendor cloud his judgment and therefore, his wisdom which was at one time perfect (v. 12) became corrupt (v. 14) and his beauty and commerce (trading of merchandise) (v. 16) became more important to him. He wanted to receive the glory of it all for himself. He wanted to be the ruler, not the ruled.

So we must understand that it is extremely important to keep our eyes focused on our Creator God, not on ourselves, our beauty, our wisdom, possessions, gifts or talents. By focusing on these things more than God, we open up the door of our heart to pride which breeds deception.

Obadiah 1:3:

³"The pride of your heart has deceived you,
  You who dwell in the clefts of the rock,
whose habitation is high; you who say in your heart, 'Who will bring me down to the ground?'"

We open up the door for our hearts to be lifted up.

Examples: Look at how big and beautiful our church building is. Look at all the people I've prayed for who were saved, healed and delivered. Look at how nice my car is. I sure hope they notice my new suit, tie and snakeskin boots. After all, they need to remember who I am. I'm so proud of the revelation God gave me. I have great wisdom and they need to listen to me.

Our church is the only church that's doing anything for God, etc. Are you getting the picture? God is not against us having nice things as long as we remember who gave them to us and *from whence we came.*

Psalm 40:1-4:

¹I waited patiently for the LORD;
  And He inclined to me,

> *And heard my cry.*
> *²He also <u>brought me up out</u> of a horrible pit,*
>   *Out of the miry clay,*
>   *And set my feet upon a rock,*
>   *And established my steps.*
> *³He has put a new song in my mouth—*
>   *Praise to our God;*
>   *Many will see it and fear,*
>   *And will trust in the LORD.*
> *⁴Blessed is that man who makes the LORD his trust,*
>   *And does not respect the proud, nor such as turn aside to lies.*

Ezekiel 28:17 KJV:

> *¹⁷Thine heart was lifted up because of thy beauty, thou hast corrupted thy wisdom by reason of thy brightness: <u>I will cast thee to the ground</u>, I will lay thee before kings, that they may behold thee.*

We also see the results of lifting ourselves up. We will be cast down. Let's remember to give God the glory, the credit for our accomplishments, beauty and splendor that He bestows upon us.

Let's take another look at the subtlety of pride. Read Genesis, chapter 3, verses 1-5 KJV:

> *¹Now the serpent was more <u>subtil</u> than any beast of the field which the LORD God had made. And he said unto the woman, Yea, hath God said, Ye shall not eat of every tree of the garden? ²And the woman said unto the serpent, We may eat of the fruit of the trees of the garden:*

> *³But of the fruit of the tree which is in the midst of the garden, God hath said, Ye shall not eat of it, neither shall ye touch it, lest ye die.*
> *⁴And the serpent said unto the woman, Ye shall not surely die: ⁵For God doth know that in the day ye eat thereof, then your eyes shall be opened, and ye shall be as gods, knowing good and evil.*

The word "subtle" ("subtil" in the *King James Version*) in verse 1 means crafty, prudence, to imitate cunning plans, to be crafty. Notice in verse 1 that the serpent was using his craftiness, his subtlety in the form of a question, but not just a question; a question concerning what God had spoken to Adam and Eve. So we see that he even had the craftiness to bring God into the picture. Why? Because God is the One who had spoken to Adam and Eve and he, the serpent, wanted to get back at God because of what happened to him. He wanted a place of position again (v. 14). We see that the serpent was questioning the authority of God's word to Adam and Eve. He (the serpent) was doing his best to try and get them to ultimately disobey God's spoken words to them. He knew if he could get them to disobey the Word of God that he could and would cause them to fall and relinquish their God-given authority. In other words, God had given them specific instructions, but they decided to obey the serpent's instructions instead of God's. This we must come to understand is a subtle form of pride. Again, we must realize that both Adam and Eve knew what God had told them, but they willingly sinned by disobeying Him. However, God still loved Adam and Eve.

What is willful disobedience?

It is <u>knowing</u> in our hearts what God has been telling us to do or not to do, but as an act of our will, we do it or don't do it anyway. This type of willful disobedience opens the door for our adversary to take control in our lives. Willful disobedience actually stems from a stubborn and rebellious heart.

1 Samuel 15:22-23:

²²So Samuel said:
  "Has the LORD as great delight in burnt offerings and sacrifices,
    As in obeying the voice of the LORD?
    Behold, to obey is better than sacrifice,
    And to heed than the fat of rams.
²³For rebellion is as the sin of witchcraft,
    And stubbornness is as iniquity and idolatry
  Because you have rejected the word of the LORD,
    He also has rejected you from being king."

Remember this: Stubbornness and pride go hand in hand. A submissive, teachable heart and humility go hand in hand.

We have seen in the previous chapters how pride begins or how it takes root in a person's heart. Now let's take a look at the sinful results of pride in one's heart and life.

The Bible tells us in Matthew 7:17, *"Even so, every good tree bears good fruit, but a bad tree bears bad fruit."* So if in the soil of our heart we have allowed a seed of pride to be planted, there will be certain fruit that will show up or spring forth to prove it.

1 John 2:15-17:

¹⁵Do not love the world or the things in the world. If anyone loves the world, the love of the Father is not in him. ¹⁶For all *that is in the world—the lust of the flesh, the lust of the eyes, and the <u>pride of life</u>—is <u>not</u> of the Father but is <u>of the world</u>. ¹⁷And the <u>world is passing away, and the lust of it</u>; but he who does the will of God abides forever.*

As we see here in this passage of scripture, pride is not part of God's will, but the will of the world.

Proverbs 8:13:

The fear of the Lord is to hate evil; pride and arrogance and the evil way and the perverse mouth I hate.

CHAPTER 5

RESULTS OF A PRIDEFUL HEART

1. Pride Precedes Captivity.

Jeremiah 13:15-18:

¹⁵Hear and give ear:
   <u>Do not be proud,</u>
   For the LORD has spoken.
¹⁶Give glory to the LORD your God
   Before He causes darkness,
   And before your feet stumble
   On the dark mountains,
   And while you are looking for light,
   He turns it into the shadow of death
   And makes it dense darkness.
¹⁷But if you will not hear it,
   My soul will weep in secret for your pride;
   My eyes will weep bitterly
   And run down with tears,
   Because the LORD's flock has been taken captive.
¹⁸Say to the king and to the queen mother,

"Humble yourselves; sit down, for your rule shall collapse, the crown of your glory."

2. Pride Causes God to Weep.

Pride takes and keeps God's people away from His presence and brings them into captivity.

Jeremiah 13:17:

¹⁷But if you will not hear it, my soul will weep in secret for your pride; my eyes will weep bitterly, and run down with tears, because the LORD's flock has been taken captive.

Ezekiel 18:23-32:

²³"Do I have any pleasure at all that the wicked should die?" says the Lord GOD, "and not that he should turn from his ways and live?
²⁴"But when a righteous man turns away from his righteousness and commits iniquity, and does according to all the abominations that the wicked man does, shall he live? All the righteousness which he has done shall not be remembered; because of the unfaithfulness of which he is guilty and the sin which he has committed, because of them he shall die.
²⁵"Yet you say, 'The way of the Lord is not fair.' Hear now, O house of Israel, is it not My way which is fair, and your ways which are not fair? ²⁶When a righteous man turns away from his righteousness, commits iniquity, and dies in it, it is because of the iniquity which he has done that he dies. ²⁷Again, when a wicked man turns away from the wickedness which he committed, and does what is lawful and right, he preserves himself alive. ²⁸Because he considers and turns away from all the transgressions which he committed, he shall surely live; he shall not die. ²⁹Yet the

house of Israel says, 'The way of the Lord is not fair.' O house of Israel, is it not My ways which are fair, and your ways which are not fair?
³⁰"Therefore I will judge you, O house of Israel, every one according to his ways," says the Lord GOD. "<u>Repent, and turn from all your transgressions, so that iniquity will not be your ruin</u>. ³¹Cast away from you all the transgressions which you have committed, and get yourselves a new heart and a new spirit. For why should you die, O house of Israel? ³²For <u>I have no pleasure in the death of one who dies," says the Lord GOD</u>. "Therefore turn and live!"

Ezekiel 33:11:

¹¹"Say to them: 'As I live,' says the Lord GOD, 'I have no pleasure in the death of the wicked, but that the wicked turn from his way and live. Turn, turn from your evil ways! For why should you die, O house of Israel?'"

3. Pride Opens the Door for Deception.

We end up deceived in our own hearts. If a deceived person knew he was deceived, he wouldn't be deceived. Selah. So to counteract deception, we must by an act of our will remain teachable and humble before God.

Obadiah 1:3:

³"The pride of your heart has deceived you,
  You who dwell in the clefts of the rock,
  Whose habitation is high;
  You who say in your heart, 'Who will bring me down to the ground?'"

4. **Pride Defiles Us, Pollutes Us, Makes Us Profane or Unclean.**

   Mark 7: 21-23:

   ^{21}*"For from within, out of the heart of men, proceed evil thoughts, adulteries, fornications, murders, ^{22}thefts, covetousness, wickedness, deceit, lewdness, an evil eye, blasphemy, pride, foolishness. ^{23}All these evil things come from within and defile a man."*

5. **Pride Causes Us to Fall into Condemnation.**

   1 Timothy 3:6:

   ^{6}*Not a novice, lest being puffed up with pride he fall into the same condemnation as the devil.*

6. **Pride Causes Shame.**

   Proverbs 11:2:

   ^{2}*When pride comes, then comes shame; but with the humble is wisdom.*

   Shame – Disgrace, confusion, dishonor, reproach.

   Disgrace – Falling away from God's grace because we are doing our own thing, following our own ways.

7. **Pride Causes Contention.**

   Proverbs 13:10:

   ^{10}*By pride comes nothing but strife, but with the well-advised is wisdom.*

   Contention, which means to quarrel, debate, to bring strife, to be expelled, to be desolate, to be laid waste.

(Husbands and wives, it is not about having your own way, but having God's way.)

8. **Pride Provides a Foolish Mouth.**

    Proverbs 14:3:

    ³In the mouth of a fool is a rod of pride, but the lips of the wise will preserve them.

    Foolish means a perverse mouth, to distort, misinterpret or corrupt, turn away. We end up distorting the scriptures to our advantage or what we believe is right.

9. **Pride Brings Destruction.**

    Proverbs 16:18:

    ¹⁸Pride goes before destruction, and a haughty spirit before a fall.

    Destruction means a fracture, ruin, affliction, breach, a breaking, bruise, crashing, hurt, vexation, break down, off or in pieces. (References: Isaiah 9:8-13, Ezekiel 7:10, Proverbs 15:25.)

10. **Pride Brings Us Low.**

    Proverbs 29:23:

    ²³A man's pride will bring him low, but the humble in spirit will retain honor.

    "Low" means to be cast down, humbled, brought lower, abase. (Reference: 1 Corinthians 10:12.)

11. **Pride Is Going to Pass Away.**

    1 John 2:15-17:

    ¹⁵Do not love the world or the things in the world. If anyone loves the world, the love of the Father is not in him. ¹⁶For all that is in the world—the lust of the flesh, the lust of the eyes, and the pride of life—is not of the Father but is of the world. [17]And the world is passing away, and the lust of it; but he who does the will of God abides forever.

Pride is of this world, not of God. Only those things which are of God will remain.

12. **Demotion May Happen as a Result of Our Pride.**

Daniel 5:18-20:

[18]"O king, the Most High God gave Nebuchadnezzar your father a kingdom and majesty, glory and honor. [19]And because of the majesty that He gave him, all peoples, nations, and languages trembled and feared before him. Whomever he wished, he executed; whomever he wished, he kept alive; whomever he wished, he set up; and whomever he wished, he put down. [20]But <u>when his heart was lifted up, and his spirit was hardened in pride</u>, he was deposed <u>from his kingly throne, and they took his glory from him</u>."

Our minds eventually become hardened. Pharaoh's mind was also hardened because of his pride. (References: Exodus 8:32, 9:34.) He wouldn't listen to God who was speaking through Moses.

13. **Pride Is a Bad Testimony and Produces a Bad Testimony of Character.**

Hosea 5:1-5:

[1]"Hear this, O priests! Take heed, O house of Israel! Give ear, O house of the king! For yours is the judgment, because you have been a snare to Mizpah and a net spread on Tabor. [2]The revolters are deeply involved in slaughter, though I

rebuke them all. ³*I know Ephraim, and Israel is not hidden from Me; for now, O Ephraim, you commit harlotry; Israel is defiled.*
⁴*They do not direct their deeds, toward turning to their God,*
   For the spirit of harlotry is in their midst, and they do not know the LORD.
⁵<u>*The pride of Israel testifies to his face;*</u>
   therefore Israel and Ephraim stumble in their iniquity; Judah also stumbles with them."

14. Pride Produces Unhealthy Competition.

1 Samuel 18:1-16:

¹*Now when he had finished speaking to Saul, the soul of Jonathan was knit to the soul of David, and Jonathan loved him as his own soul.* ²*Saul took him that day, and would not let him go home to his father's house anymore.* ³*Then Jonathan and David made a covenant, because he loved him as his own soul.* ⁴*And Jonathan took off the robe that was on him and gave it to David, with his armor, even to his sword and his bow and his belt.*
⁵*So David went out wherever Saul sent him, and behaved wisely. And Saul set him over the men of war, and he was accepted in the sight of all the people and also in the sight of Saul's servants.* ⁶*Now it had happened as they were coming home, when David was returning from the slaughter of the Philistine, that the women had come out of all the cities of Israel, singing and dancing, to meet King Saul, with tambourines, with joy, and with musical instruments.* ⁷*So the women sang as they danced, and said:*

   "<u>*Saul has slain his thousands,*</u>
   <u>*And David his ten thousands.*</u>"

⁸Then Saul was very angry, and the saying displeased him; and he said, "They have ascribed to David ten thousands, and to me they have ascribed only thousands. Now what more can he have but the kingdom?" ⁹So Saul eyed David from that day forward. ¹⁰And it happened on the next day that the distressing spirit from God came upon Saul, and he prophesied inside the house. So David played music with his hand, as at other times; but there was a spear in Saul's hand. ¹¹And Saul cast the spear, for he said, "I will pin David to the wall!" But David escaped his presence twice.

¹²Now Saul was afraid of David, because the LORD was with him, but had departed from Saul. ¹³Therefore Saul removed him from his presence, and made him his captain over a thousand; and he went out and came in before the people. ¹⁴And David behaved wisely in all his ways, and the LORD was with him. ¹⁵Therefore, when Saul saw that he behaved very wisely, he was afraid of him. ¹⁶But all Israel and Judah loved David, because he went out and came in before them.

Pride produces unhealthy competition, which can produce attitudes of jealous rage and thoughts of destruction. Saul allowed pride into his heart and sought to kill David because of it.

Other examples or attitudes of unhealthy competition would be having to have the biggest and most beautiful church building, drive the nicest car, have the most fancy clothes, preach the most dynamic sermons with the most eloquent speech, sing better than anyone else, have the biggest, best choir with the nicest robes, outgive everyone else, do more than anyone else, bake the perfect apple pie, make the best quilt, write the most books, etc.

All of these attitudes stem from a heart of pride based on wrong motives. Our real concerns should be, are we winning souls for Jesus' sake, healing the sick, casting out devils, setting people free and doing the work of God in the earth!

15. Pride Causes Us to Reject the Word of God When It's Delivered to Us.

Exodus 5:1-2:

¹Afterward Moses and Aaron went in and told Pharaoh, "Thus says the LORD God of Israel: 'Let My people go, that they may hold a feast to Me in the wilderness.'"
²And Pharaoh said, "<u>Who is the LORD, that I should obey His voice</u> to let Israel go? <u>I do not know the LORD, nor will I let Israel go.</u>"

In Hosea 4:6 they rejected knowledge and God rejected them because of it.

16. Pride Brings Rebuke from God, a Curse into Our Lives and Causes Us to Err and Stray from God's Word.

Psalm 119:21:

²¹You rebuke the proud—the cursed, who stray from Your commandments.

17. Pride Causes Us to be an Abomination Unto God and Results in Punishment.

Proverbs 16:5:

⁵Everyone proud in heart is an abomination to the LORD; though they join forces, none will go unpunished.

Hebrew for "abomination" means a detestable thing, a loathsome thing, to be repulsive, vile and rejected. Remember the vision of the hand in chapter 1. (References James 4:6; 1 Peter 5:5.)

I have just listed seventeen biblical negative results of pride. Our loving Heavenly Father wants us to walk humbly before Him so that none of those things will come upon us. He wants us to continually walk humbly before Him so that we will be able to stand against Satan and his demonic forces in the last days. Pride opens the door for Satan to deceive us in <u>every</u> area of life. Even now, as you are reading this book, many Christian leaders, churches, Christian men and women, are falling and being destroyed because of the sin of pride. The sad thing is, most of them don't even realize it because it's so deceptive and subtle.

Remember in the previous chapter it was stated that if a deceived person knew they were deceived, they wouldn't be deceived.

Think about it! How many leaders, ministries and Christians in the Body of Christ have fallen even after being confronted by their friends or peers in the ministry concerning false doctrines that they were teaching or maybe about character issues that needed changing but they weren't willing to deal with them? What good is it to claim that we are submitted to those whom God has placed in authority over us if when we are confronted we refuse to listen? That means we're unteachable and walking in pride.

It's hard to get through to a deceived person because they don't believe they are deceived. Therefore, they usually refuse instruction or correction. Sometimes all we can do is to continue to pray for them.

Do you see how devastating pride is and why God hates it and why it is an abomination unto Him? He doesn't want us to fall. He wants us to stand and run the race set before us and finish our course. He wants us to fulfill our destiny in Him. He loves us so much, and because of His love, He warns us of issues such as pride in our lives.

Again, Proverbs 8:13 reminds us, *"The fear of the LORD is to hate evil; pride and arrogance and the evil way and the perverse mouth I hate."*

So if we as Christians really have a fear of the Lord in our lives, <u>we will hate pride</u> because pride is evil and it's something God hates. We must learn to love what God loves and learn to hate what He hates. It's not up to God to keep us humble, it's up to us!

CHAPTER 6

SAFEGUARDING OUR HEARTS FROM THE SIN OF PRIDE

Now that we've seen the importance of keeping our hearts free from the sin of pride, let's talk about <u>how</u> we can safeguard our hearts from it.

First, let me share with you how the Lord taught me to fear Him so that I would develop a hatred in my heart for pride and sin in general.

In 1986 I began to call upon the Lord in prayer, asking Him to help me hate evil so that I wouldn't put up with it in my own life and so that I could also help others overcome evil in their lives. The Holy Spirit led me to Isaiah 11:1-3. This would be the beginning of answers to my prayer concerning this subject.

Isaiah 11:1-3:

> *¹There shall come forth a Rod from the stem of Jesse,*
> *and a Branch shall grow out of his roots.*
> *²The Spirit of the LORD shall rest upon Him,*

> *The Spirit of wisdom and understanding,*
> *The Spirit of counsel and might,*
> *The Spirit of knowledge and of the fear of the LORD.*
> *³<u>His delight is in the fear of the LORD</u>,*
> *And He shall not judge by the sight of His eyes,*
> *Nor decide by the hearing of His ears.*

Notice in verse 3 that His (Jesus) delight would be to walk in the fear of the Lord.

Again, Proverbs 8:13 says that *if we truly fear the Lord we will hate pride.* We can surely see that Jesus hated pride. No wonder He was continually confronted, ridiculed, mocked and scorned by the prideful religious leaders of His day. Their pride was attacking His humility, His submitted heart to the Father.

The Bible says in Philippians 2:8, *"He [Jesus] <u>humbled Himself and became obedient</u> to the point of death, even the death on the cross."* Jesus walked in humility by an act of His own will. <u>He chose</u> to walk <u>humbly</u> before His Father in heaven. Also out of His heart of humility came obedience to His Father's will, not His own will!

Because Jesus developed a fear of the Lord in His life, He developed a hatred toward anything and everything evil which included pride and religious pride in particular. The results were that He was able then to live a victorious and humble life, totally obedient to His Father's will.

SAFEGUARDS

The very <u>first thing</u> I did to help safeguard my heart against pride was to <u>call upon the Holy Spirit's ministry of teaching me and developing in me a fear of the Lord</u>.

I remember asking the Holy Spirit to rise up big within me to hate evil so that I wouldn't put up with it in my own life and would be able to help others to whom I would be ministering.

In all seriousness, you and I most likely aren't going to deal with anything we don't hate. We'll probably just tolerate it in our lives, which means if we don't develop a hatred for pride, we'll put up with it in our lives pretending that it's not a big deal. Just remember, however, *it's the little foxes that spoil the vine* (*see* Song of Solomon 2:15).

The second way to safeguard against pride is to guard our minds by resisting prideful thoughts of exaltation and by keeping the attitude of a servant, which is the mind of Christ.

Philippians 2:5-7:

⁵Let this mind be in you which was also in Christ Jesus, ⁶who, being in the form of God, did not consider it robbery to be equal with God, ⁷but made Himself of no reputation, taking the form of a bondservant, and coming in the likeness of men.

Yes, we are sons and daughters of God, but sons and daughters of God have servant hearts.

The third way to safeguard our hearts against pride is to stay submitted and accountable to those in authority over us. To humble ourselves through willful submission means that by an act of our will, we put ourselves under God's established authority for our lives. Each of us must find out who that authority is. Submitting to godly authority means to remain teachable at all times; to be open for rebukes, reproof and correction also. Even the Apostle Paul said, *"Imitate me, just as I also imitate Christ"* (1 Corinthians 11:1).

What I have experienced as a pastor is that there is a big difference between verbal submission and actual submission. We all know that our flesh wants to be in control and never wants to willfully receive correction when needed. In other words, it's one thing to say we're submitted to godly authority, but another thing to receive correction when we are truly needing it.

Pastors and leaders in the Body of Christ find out real quick who's really with them or against them when it comes to confronting those who need to be confronted, in the love of the Lord, of course.

The other side of the coin is the question of whether the pastors and leaders in the Body of Christ are truly open to correction from those in authority over them (if there is someone whom they are truly accountable to). It's sad to say, but there are a lot of lone rangers, maverick churches and ministries. A prideful heart never wants to be corrected or even challenged for that matter. <u>However, you do not have to and are not obligated to submit to those in authority over you if they are telling you to do things that are contrary to God's Word</u>. We always obey God's Word first and foremost! Also, make sure you keep your heart right by loving and by praying for your pastor and those in leadership.

The <u>fourth way</u> to safeguard your heart is to <u>rightly divide God's Word</u>.

You might say, "How is that going to safeguard my heart from pride?" When we take a particular scripture <u>out of its setting</u> and establish a doctrine out of it for our own convenience, that's pride and we open up the door for deception.

It's amazing how many Christians have established a doctrine on a half-truth and became proud of it. They became proud of their so-called newfound revelation, and it's difficult to convince them otherwise.

<u>Remember to check your revelation out with those in authority</u> over you, especially before you teach it publicly. Checking it out with others will help safeguard your heart against what I call revelatory pride (being proud of your revelation) which may not be an accurate revelation at all.

2 Timothy 2:15:

¹⁵Be diligent to present yourself approved to God, a worker who does not need to be ashamed, <u>rightly dividing</u> the word of truth.

The <u>fifth way</u> to safeguard your heart is to <u>remain in God's presence through the reading and study of His Word, personal worship, and praying in the Holy Ghost</u>. By staying in His presence we will develop in us His character of humility.

The <u>sixth way</u> to safeguard your heart is to <u>speak God's Word over yourself</u>! Example: As an act of my will, I humble myself today, Father, under Your mighty hand! I walk humbly before my God (James 1:10).

Why do we need to speak these things?

Because Romans 10:17 KJV says that *"Faith cometh by hearing, and hearing by the word of God."* I'm expressing my faith in God's Word by speaking God's Word concerning my desire and His will for me to walk in humility.

Mark 11:22-23:

^{22}*So Jesus answered and said to them, "Have faith in God. ^{23}For assuredly, I say to you, whoever says to this mountain, 'Be removed and be cast into the sea,' and does not doubt in his heart, but believes that those things he says will be done, <u>he will have whatever he says</u>."*

Also, pride will become a huge mountain in our lives if it goes unchecked or unresisted by us.

Religious traditions of men have taught us that it is God who humbles us when we need it. However, the problem with this teaching or thought is that it is always God's will for us to be humble. So if God is the One who humbles us and it is always His will for us to be humble, we would all be humble all of the time.

We must understand that when God made each of us, He gave us a free will. So it is our choice whether we choose to humble ourselves or have a prideful heart and attitude. God already determined what His choice or will is for us. His choice is for us to humble ourselves under His authority or mighty hand so that as we humble ourselves, <u>He</u>, <u>not us</u>, can exalt us in due time.

Do you see the difference? Lucifer exalted himself by an act of his will instead of humbling himself and allowing God to exalt him. When <u>he said, "I will exalt myself,"</u> he was cast down.

Did you notice what he did? He <u>said</u>, "I will." Don't forget to watch out for the <u>Big I</u> (your own will)!

The Lord spoke to me in a worship service years ago, and said, "It's time that My people get honest with Me and with one another, for honesty is the prerequisite to every type of healing that they need."

Remember 2 Chronicles 7:14:

The Lord said that if His people which are called by His name would <u>humble</u> <u>themselves</u> and pray and seek His face and turn from their wicked ways, <u>then and only then</u> would He <u>hear</u> from heaven, <u>forgive</u> their sins and <u>heal</u> their land.

Godly humility produces godly honesty! Without honesty (getting honest in our own hearts before God) we'll just keep going around the same mountain and wonder why our situations and circumstances just aren't changing. Could it possibly be that we are still hanging onto a little pride, not wanting to admit our sins, our mistakes, our bad attitudes and ought towards others? Could it be that we're thinking that <u>if we admit</u> that <u>we missed it</u> and even blew it big time, what are those around us going to think?

James 5:16 KJV says, *"Confess your faults one to another, and pray one for another, that ye may be healed. The effectual fervent prayer of a righteous man availeth much."*

You see, if what others might think is your or my concern, we are still struggling with a fear of man which leads us to follow man and not God.

I will admit to you today that the greatest times of restoration in my life came only through the channel of admitting my sins and my shortcomings (that's true, godly humility). That's what God desires: admittance and repentance. Having pastored two churches, I came to realize that most of God's people were very forgiving and receptive when I openly admitted my mistakes. Most people do like transparent, honest preachers, however, too many Christians put their leaders on a pedestal, expecting them to be perfect and sinless. This is not a good thing to do. No one is perfect or sinless but God!

There are also far too many ministers living behind glass doors, afraid of having their doors shattered. Don't ever hide behind the door of pride. Confess your sins immediately, and admit your faults. This will close the door on pride. Pride must come down and humility must come in.

I learned over the years, particularly from other minister friends, that most everything starts at the head, and then filters down through the body. If we want church people who walk humbly before God, we as ministers of God must set the example and walk humbly before Him. If we don't want our church people gossiping, then we need to stop gossiping and being a busybody. To expect God's people to do something different, or act differently than we do, is called hypocrisy, a double standard.

Let me ask all of you fellow ministers a question. In your church, are you willing to go to that person whom you have offended? Or do you just expect those who have offended you to come to you because you're the pastor, the leader in charge?

I've learned that most people can see right through us and that sheep really aren't as dumb as we think. As a matter of fact, what I have observed is that many of God's sheep are more discerning than many of God's shepherds because many of God's shepherds are deceived as a result of the pride in their own hearts and lives. This is the truth! We as God's shepherds and ministers must humble ourselves and stay humble before God so that we end up leading, feeding and guiding

God's sheep instead of beating them, misleading them, manipulating them and controlling them. Jesus loves His sheep and He laid down His life for them.

Today we have too many shepherds who have not truly laid down their lives for God's sheep. They are still feeding themselves and many of them are hirelings. Do you know who the hirelings are? They're the shepherds who run when the pressure is on, when things aren't going so well or going their way, or when they see the wolf coming.

John 10:11-13:

11"I am the good shepherd. The good shepherd gives His life for the sheep. 12But a hireling, he who is not the shepherd, one who does not own the sheep, sees the wolf coming and leaves the sheep and flees; and the wolf catches the sheep and scatters them. 13The hireling flees because he is a hireling and does not care about the sheep."

True shepherds fight for the sheep. The true shepherd speaks the truth and refuses to compromise the teaching of God's Word. True shepherds love the sheep unconditionally. True shepherds go after the one lost sheep, leaving the 99. This is the God-kind of love and humility!

Humility serves. Pride wants to be served and is demanding. This is why Jesus humbled Himself and took on the form of a servant. True shepherds are protectors of the sheep. They care more about the welfare of the sheep than their own welfare. How sad it must have been for Jesus to see the sheep scattered and having no shepherd.

It's time for <u>all of God's people</u> to <u>truly</u> (humble themselves), especially those in leadership positions because we are to be examples. Jesus said in John 10:27, *"My sheep hear My voice, and I know them, and they follow Me."* Are the sheep hearing the voice of pride or the voice of humility from their shepherds and leaders? Are they observing attitudes of pride or humility? Are you as a Christian walking with a humble heart, submitted to godly authority, mainly your pastor?

Ephesians 5:21 says that we are all supposed to submit one to another in the fear of the Lord. Doing this will help us maintain a humble heart and will help maintain unity in our churches and homes.

Closing Thoughts

Many years ago as I was traveling and ministering, I heard the Lord say to me, "I am more interested in character than charisma."

Paul said in 1 Corinthians 13:4 that *God's love* (which is the first fruit of the Spirit) *is not boastful or proud.* Verse 5 in the *Amplified Bible* says, *God's love is not inflated with pride.*

So the Lord was saying to me that He was more interested in the character of love and humility than charisma. The fruit of the Spirit represents character. The gifts of the Spirit represent charisma.

Character is what we're made of – it stabilizes our lives. *Love, joy, peace, longsuffering, kindness, gentleness, faithfulness, goodness and self-control* (see Galatians 5:22-23). These make up our character. I heard it said that some people have character and some are characters.

You and I can be operating in charisma (the gifts of the Spirit) and not be developed in the character of God. The church at Corinth proved that. They operated in the gifts but lacked love (character).

So let's remember to keep first things first. If we're walking in God's love, it's impossible to be haughty, boastful and puffed up with pride.

I don't know all the reasons why the subject of pride has not been taught on more often. I suppose one reason may be because Satan has tried his best to stop it. He knows when God's people get a revelation of true godly humility, they will be exalted and lifted up above him and his demonic forces. They will walk all over him!

There is great strength in <u>godly</u> humility. Satan knows that humility will help God's people to stand against him, but pride will cause God's people to fall in self-defeat with him.

Remember: In order for Satan to get you and me to fall, he has to first get us to exalt ourselves by an act of our will. Don't give in to his trickery and pray that you enter not into the temptation of the sin of pride. Matthew 26:41 says, *"Watch and pray, lest you enter into temptation. The spirit indeed is willing, but the flesh is weak."*

Remember to <u>humble yourself</u> under the mighty hand of God and He (God) will exalt you, <u>not resist you,</u> in due time (1 Peter 5:1-8).

I hope you enjoyed this book and that it ministered to your heart. I pray that it has made you more aware of Satan's subtlety of pride. We all must beware of the subtleties of pride so that we will fulfill all that God has for us to do. Satan has taken captive many of our fellow ministers and brothers and sisters and knocked them out of the race through the deceitfulness of pride.

Let's remember to pray for those who have slipped and fallen and do our best to restore them back into fellowship with Jesus, the Author and Finisher of their faith. First Corinthians 10:17 says, *"For we, though many, are one bread and one body; for we all partake of that one bread."*

Galatians 6:1:

¹Brethren, if a man is overtaken in any trespass, you who are spiritual restore such a one in a spirit of gentleness, considering yourself lest you also be tempted.

As we go forth to restore them, let's remember to do this in a spirit of meekness lest we fall into the same temptation.

Galatians 6:2-5:

²Bear one another's burdens, and so fulfill the law of Christ. ³For <u>if anyone thinks himself to be something, when he is nothing, he deceives himself</u>. 4 But let each one examine his own work, and then he will have rejoicing in himself alone, and not in another. 5 For each one shall bear his own load.

CHRISTIAN PRAYER

If you through the reading of this book have recognized areas of ungodly pride in your life and sincerely want to change and begin to walk humbly before God, pray this prayer with a sincere heart:

Heavenly Father, I thank You for revealing to me areas of my life that I've been prideful in, even to the point of exalting myself, wanting to do things my way and not Yours. I repent of the sin of pride and ask that You would forgive me. I desire to fulfill my calling and Your plan for my life, Lord Jesus. Holy Spirit, I ask that You would open up my eyes and ears to Satan's temptations of pride and that You would help me to maintain a humble heart and attitude. As an act of my will, I humble myself under the mighty hand of God right now so that He can and will exalt me in due time. Thank You, Heavenly Father, for forgiving me, loving me and for being merciful to me. AMEN.

Sinner's Prayer

The Bible says in Romans chapter 10 verses 9 and 10 that if you confess with your mouth the Lord Jesus Christ and believe in your heart that God has raised Him from the dead, thou shalt be saved; for with the heart man believes unto righteousness and with the mouth confession is made unto salvation.

If you have never accepted Jesus Christ as your Lord and Savior and would like to today, pray this prayer in sincerity to God:

Heavenly Father, I realize that my life without You is hopeless. I've been going the wrong way, living for me, not for You, and I'm asking Jesus to come into my life and save me from my sins. I want to go to heaven when I die or when Jesus returns. I thank You for loving me and saving me today. Now I don't have to worry about where I'll be spending eternity. I know it will be with You. AMEN.

If you prayed either of these prayers, would you please let me know by emailing <u>lwalkministries@yahoo.com</u>. I would appreciate knowing how my book changed your life.

Don't ever forget that God loves you unconditionally and always forgives you when you are sincere in your heart in asking for forgiveness. Zephaniah 3 verse 17 in the Amplified Bible says this quote: The Lord your God is in the midst of you, a Mighty One, a Savior who saves. He will rejoice over you with joy: He will rest in silent satisfaction and in His love He will be silent and make No mention of past sins, or even recall them: He will exalt over you with singing.

I pray that this book has touched your heart in one way or another and that you will follow your Lord and Savior Jesus Christ the rest of your life, allowing Him to continue to work in you and through you to reach this lost and dying world for Him!

Sincerely in His Service,
Charles R. Sund

Scripture References

Here are a few more references for the words "pride," "proud" and "proudly" to further your own study.

Nehemiah 9:16, 29
Psalm 10:2, 4, 18:27, 31:23, 36:11-12, 59:12, 73:6, 94:2
Proverbs 8:13, 11:2, 13:10, 14:3, 16:18, 29:23
Isaiah 9:9, 16:6, 23:9, 25:11, 28:1, 3
Jeremiah 13:9, 48:29
Ezekiel 16:56, 30:6
Daniel 5:20
Hosea 5:5
Obadiah 1:3
Zephaniah 2:10-11, 9:6, 10:11
Malachi 4:1
Mark 7:22
Romans 1:30
Ephesians 6:13
1 Timothy 3:6
2 Timothy 3:2
James 4:6, 10
1 Peter 5:5-6
1 John 2:16

About the Author

Charles Sund accepted Jesus Christ as his Savior at the age of twelve in his hometown of Newburg, North Dakota. With the limited biblical knowledge he had concerning Satan's warfare against him, he was unable to stand against Satan's temptations to alcohol, drugs, nicotine and an ungodly lifestyle. By the age of sixteen, he was an alcoholic who was extremely depressed, lonely, brokenhearted and suicidal.

In 1980, through the love and power of God, and prayers of others who cared about him, he was supernaturally set free from addictions, suicidal tendencies, depression and loneliness.

In 1982, he was called by God out of a wonderful family-owned business to preach the gospel of Christ. Along with his wife, Nancy, he attended RHEMA Bible Training Center in Broken Arrow, Oklahoma, where he graduated in 1984.

Charles and Nancy Sund reside in Fargo, North Dakota. They have been married thirty-nine years and have two wonderful daughters and six awesome grandkids.

Lovewalk Ministries is a ministry of edification, exhortation and comfort; preaching and teaching the uncompromised Word of God with signs following.

To purchase books, for more information,
or to schedule Charles Sund to minister,
please contact:

Charles Sund

<u>lwalkministries@yahoo.com</u>

Additional copies of *Help Me I'm Falling!* are also available at fine bookstores everywhere.